Lenny Wilkens

THE STORY OF THE OKLAHOMA CITY THUNDER

Luguentz Dort

A HISTORY OF HOOPS

THE STORY OF THE

OKLAHOMA CITY THUNDER

JIM WHITING

Dennis Johnson

CREATIVE EDUCATION / CREATIVE PAPERBACKS

Published by Creative Education and Creative Paperbacks
P.O. Box 227, Mankato, Minnesota 56002
Creative Education and Creative Paperbacks are imprints of
The Creative Company
www.thecreativecompany.us

Design and production by Blue Design (www.bluedes.com)
Art direction by Rita Marshall

Photographs by Alamy (Zuma Press Inc.), AP Images (David Zalubowski),
Corbis (Mike Segar), Getty (Lachlan Cunningham, Tim DeFrisco, James Drake,
Focus On Sport, Sean Gardner, Thearon W. Henderson, Ron Hoskins, John
Iacono, George Long, Melissa Majchrzak, Fernando Medina, Manny Millan,
NBA Photo Library, Abbie Parr, Mike Powell, Dick Raphael, Rogers Photo
Archive, Patrick Smith, Matthew Stockman, Rocky Widner), © Steve Lipofsky,
Newscom (Jeff Lewis/Icon SMI, Ting Shen/Xinhua/Photoshot), USPresswire
(David Butler II)

Library of Congress Cataloging-in-Publication Data
Names: Whiting, Jim, 1943- author.
Title: The story of the Oklahoma City Thunder / by Jim Whiting.
Description: Mankato, Minnesota : Creative Education and Creative
   Paperbacks, 2023. | Series: Creative Sports: A History of Hoops |
   Includes index. | Audience: Ages 8-12 |
   Audience: Grades 4-6 | Summary: "Middle grade basketball fans are
   introduced to the extraordinary history of NBA's Oklahoma City Thunder
   with a photo-laden narrative of their greatest successes and losses"--
   Provided by publisher.
Identifiers: LCCN 2022016849 (print) | LCCN 2022016850 (ebook) | ISBN
   9781640266377 (library binding) | ISBN 9781682771938 (paperback) | ISBN
   9781640007789 (pdf)
Subjects: LCSH: Oklahoma City Thunder (Basketball team)--History--Juvenile
   literature. | Basketball--Oklahoma--Oklahoma City--History--Juvenile
   literature.
Classification: LCC GV885.52.O37 W (print) | LCC GV885.52.O37 (ebook) |
   DDC 796.323/640976638--dc23/eng/20220505
LC record available at https://lccn.loc.gov/2022016849
LC ebook record available at https://lccn.loc.gov/2022016850

Donald "Slick" Watts

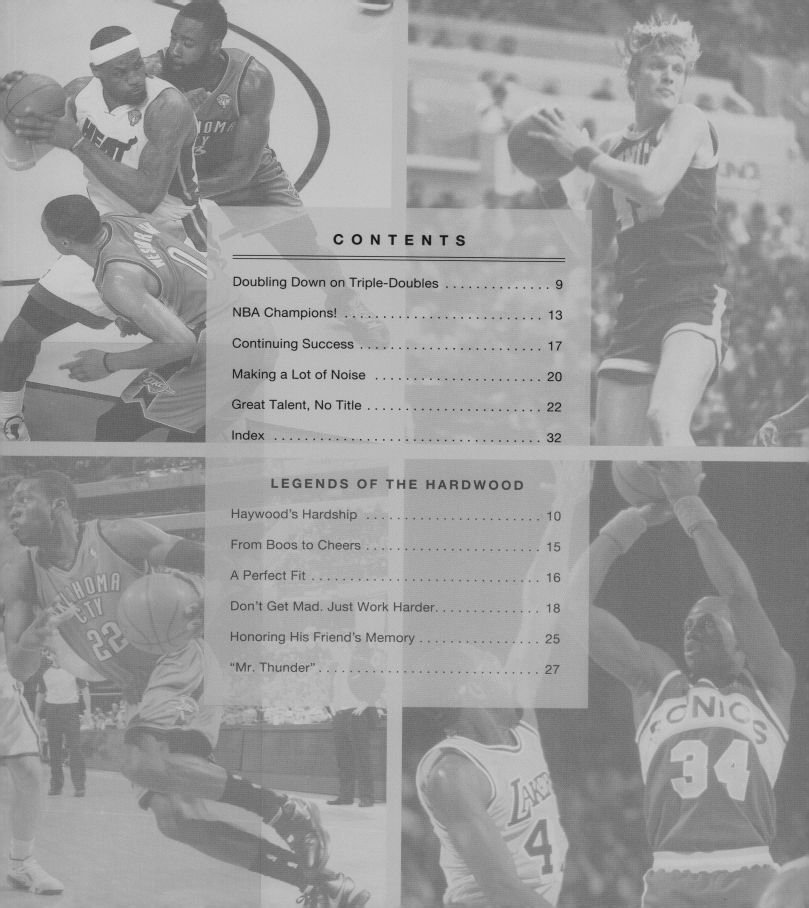

CONTENTS

LEGENDS OF THE HARDWOOD

Russell Westbrook

DOUBLING DOWN ON TRIPLE-DOUBLES

On April 9, 2017, the Oklahoma City Thunder of the National Basketball Association (NBA) traveled to Denver. The Nuggets were trying to squeeze into the playoffs. They needed every win they could get. But the crowd was focused on Thunder point guard Russell Westbrook. They wanted to see him break one of the league's oldest records.

In the 1961–62 season, Oscar Robertson, one of the greatest hoopsters of all time, had 41 games with a triple-double. That is double digits in three different statistical categories in a single game, most commonly points, rebounds, and assists. Players have to be especially versatile to achieve the feat: knock down shots, outmuscle burly big men for rebounds, and pass to teammates so they can score.

Since that season, no one had come close to Robertson's record—until now. In the season's second game, Thunder point guard Russell Westbrook had 51 points, 13 rebounds, and 13 assists. It was his first triple-double of the season. He recorded his 30th on February 28th. By then, he had become THE story of the NBA as Robertson's record now seemed to be in reach. He tied it on April 4. His teammates supported him. "He's making everybody better around him," said center Enes Kanter.

Against the Nuggets, Westbrook sat down late in the third quarter. By then he had 33 points and 14 rebounds. But he had just nine assists. When he returned

LEGENDS
OF THE HARDWOOD

SPENCER HAYWOOD
POWER FORWARD
HEIGHT: 6-FOOT-9
SONICS SEASONS: 1970–75

HAYWOOD'S HARDSHIP

Spencer Haywood played two years of college basketball. He felt he was ready for the NBA. At that time, the NBA had a rule that players couldn't be drafted until their college class had graduated. Haywood didn't want to wait. He played one year in the American Basketball Association, which didn't have the same rule as the NBA. Then the Sonics signed him, even though his class still hadn't graduated. The NBA took the Sonics to court. The Sonics successfully argued that Haywood was a "hardship case." He was the only wage earner in his large family. He had a right to earn a living playing basketball. The NBA changed its rule. College players could now be drafted if they proved financial hardship. Haywood had changed the face of pro basketball.

with nine minutes left, the crowd rose to its feet every time he touched the ball.

Nearly five minutes went by without that elusive tenth assist. Then with just over four minutes remaining, Westbrook fired a pass to point guard Semaj Christon in the right corner. Christon lofted a three-point shot. He was just a 17-percent shooter from three-point range that season. This time he sank the shot. Westbrook had broken the record!

The game was stopped as the Denver fans gave Westbrook a thunderous ovation. But the game wasn't over. With less than three seconds remaining, Denver led 105–103. Westbrook fired up an off-balance 30-foot three-point shot. It went in. Oklahoma City won 106–105. It was the perfect end to the evening. Nuggets coach Mike Malone said, "Everybody said he can't keep this up for 82 games and he has. So what he's done is something you see once in a lifetime." To underscore what Malone said, Westbrook also *averaged* a triple-double in every game that season. Robertson was the only other player who had done that.

Almost 50 years before Westbrook's record-breaking season, the Thunder began playing—in Seattle, Washington. Seattle received a franchise in late 1966. Soon afterward, the Seattle-based Boeing Company received a contract to build a supersonic transport. That contract made naming the team easy. They would be the SuperSonics, often shortened to Sonics.

At first, the Sonics didn't fly very high. The team won just 23 games in its first season of 1967–68. Wins remained hard to come by for several more seasons. But the team was assembling talent. Explosive power forward Spencer Haywood

joined Seattle in 1970. "When Spencer was on, he could demoralize the other team single-handedly," said teammate Bob Rule.

Rookie shooting/point guard Freddie Brown arrived in 1971. He was called "Downtown" because of his accurate long-range shots. Point guard Donald "Slick" Watts signed on in 1973. His gleaming bald head, lopsided green headband, and outgoing personality made him an instant fan favorite.

NBA CHAMPIONS!

Seattle made its first appearance in the playoffs in 1975. The Sonics beat the Detroit Pistons in the first round. But they fell to the Golden State Warriors in the Western Conference semifinals. They lost in the conference semifinals again the following season. After a horrendous 5–17 start in 1977–78, former player Lenny Wilkens took over as coach. He paired second-year shooting guard Dennis Johnson with point guard Gus Williams to create a formidable backcourt. The Sonics went 42–18 the rest of the season to finish 47–35 overall and advanced to the NBA Finals.

The Sonics took a 3–2 series edge over the Washington Bullets. But they couldn't hold it. In the deciding Game 7, Johnson took 14 shots. He missed them all. That tied a playoff record for most field goal attempts without a single make. The Bullets pulled out a narrow 105–99 win. "I choked," Johnson admitted. "I promised myself that I'd never repeat that performance, and as a result it made me a much stronger player."

Freddie Brown

He quickly proved how much stronger a player he was. The Sonics faced Washington in the Finals again the following season. They easily brushed aside the Bullets, winning 4 games to 1. Johnson was named Most Valuable Player (MVP) of the series. "That Sonics team was so young and talented, and it had all the makings of a dynasty," he said.

The dynasty didn't happen. Seattle won a franchise-best 56 games in 1979–80. But the Los Angeles Lakers and their superstar tandem of Kareem Abdul-Jabbar and Magic Johnson overpowered the Sonics in the Western Conference finals.

Dennis Johnson

NATE MCMILLAN
POINT GUARD
HEIGHT: 6-FOOT-5
SONICS SEASONS:
1986—98 AS PLAYER
2000—05 AS COACH

LEGENDS
OF THE HARDWOOD

FROM BOOS TO CHEERS

Seattle fans booed when the team chose Nate McMillan with
its top pick in the 1986 NBA Draft. He quickly changed their
minds. He tied a rookie record with 25 assists in a single game.
He also played smothering defense. McMillan was a Sonic for
13 seasons. Then he became head coach in 2000. McMillan led
the team to two playoff appearances. But the team wouldn't
give him a new contract. He moved to Portland to coach the
Trail Blazers. Many people think his departure marked the end
of basketball in Seattle. After he left, the team had three
losing seasons and then moved to Oklahoma City.

OKLAHOMA CITY THUNDER

15

Gary Payton

GARY PAYTON
POINT GUARD
HEIGHT: 6-FOOT-4
SONICS SEASONS:
1990–2003

A PERFECT FIT

Gary Payton was a college All-American. He was the second overall pick in the
1990 NBA Draft. He wasn't an instant star. He finally found his way during
his third season. He was especially noted for his defense. During the playoffs
that year, his cousin said, "You're holding [Phoenix Suns guard] Kevin Johnson
like a baseball in a glove." The nickname stuck. In 1996, "The Glove" became
the first point guard named Defensive Player of the Year. He was a good
shooter and passer as well. Former Los Angeles Lakers star Gail Goodrich said,
"Gary Payton is probably as complete a guard as there ever was."

The team fell apart in the following season. Williams sat it out due to a contract dispute. Johnson was traded. Several other players retired or suffered injuries. The team had just 34 wins. Seattle rebounded with three winning seasons but had early playoff exits each time. The Sonics won just 31 games in the 1984–85 season. They had the same mark in 1985–86. Rookie small forward Xavier "X-Man" McDaniel averaged 17 points and 8 rebounds per game.

Despite winning only 39 games the following season, the Sonics sneaked into the playoffs. Rookie point guard Nate McMillan quickly became a fan favorite for his team-first attitude. Seattle won the first two playoff rounds. "[Coach] Bernie [Bickerstaff] had us believing that if we walked in fire, we would come out fine, with no scratches," McDaniel said. The magical run ended in the Western Conference finals. The Lakers swept Seattle.

CONTINUING SUCCESS

The team narrowly missed the playoffs the following season. Seattle added muscular power forward Shawn Kemp in 1989. At 19, he was the youngest player in the NBA. After a slow start, he improved during the season, though the Sonics narrowly missed the playoffs. Kemp told management, "I need somebody who is going to step on this court and challenge me." That somebody turned out to be Gary Payton. The Sonics drafted him in 1990. Kemp and Payton eventually became known as the "Sonic Boom" because they played together so well.

KEVIN DURANT
SMALL FORWARD
HEIGHT: 6-FOOT-9
SONICS/THUNDER SEASONS:
2007–16

DON'T GET MAD.
JUST WORK HARDER

When Kevin Durant was young, his mother was passed over for a promotion at work. She was furious. Then she realized she hadn't worked hard enough. "I decided right then my kids would never be in the same situation," she said. "They were always going to work hard to get what they wanted." She enlisted local coach Taras Brown to make sure that would happen. "My first rule was that Kevin could never play in five-on-five pickup games," Brown said. While his buddies were playing, Durant was working with Brown on individual drills. His mother often checked up on him. If he slacked off even slightly, she made him do extra drills. The hard work paid off. Durant became the second overall pick in the 2007 NBA Draft.

George Karl became coach midway through the 1991–92 season. The "Sonic Boom" got even louder. The team surged to 55 wins the following season and advanced to the Western Conference finals. They lost to the Phoenix Suns, 4 games to 3. Fans had high hopes for the 1993–94 season. The Sonics won 63 games. That was five more than the next-best team. They had the top seed in the Western Conference. They faced Denver in the first round of the playoffs. The Nuggets had barely squeezed in as the eighth and final seed. Seattle easily won the first two games. Denver took the next three to win the series. It was one of the biggest upsets in league history. The Nuggets were the first 8-seed to knock off the top seed in the first round.

Seattle won a franchise-record 64 games in 1995–96. They faced the Chicago Bulls in the NBA Finals. The Bulls had won an NBA-record 72 games. Chicago won the first three games. No team had ever overcome a 3–0 playoff series deficit. The Sonics did their best to make history by bouncing back with a pair of double-digit wins. But Chicago won the next game to take the title.

Kemp left the following year because of a contract dispute. Karl followed him a year later. The team managed just a 25–25 mark in the lockout-shortened 1998–99 season. They posted winning records the next three seasons and twice made the playoffs. Both times they lost in the first round. The 40–42 record in 2002–03 marked Seattle's first losing record in 16 years. The following season was even worse. The Sonics won just 37 games. They rebounded to win 52 games in 2004–05. They lost to the Spurs in the conference semifinals.

MAKING A LOT OF NOISE

Three losing seasons followed. The Sonics chose small forward Kevin Durant in the 2007 NBA Draft. He became NBA Rookie of the Year. But Seattle won just 20 games. Attendance dwindled. Team owners asked Seattle city officials to build a larger arena. They refused. The owners wanted to sell the team. Oklahoma City was especially interested. It had hosted the New Orleans Hornets for two seasons after Hurricane Katrina. Fans turned out in droves to watch their adopted team. A group of Oklahoma City businessmen bought the Sonics and moved the team there in 2008.

Fans voted on 64 potential names. "Thunder" was the winner. The name honored the region's military heritage. The 45th Division of the U.S. Army had its headquarters in Oklahoma City before being deactivated in 1968. The division's nickname was Thunderbirds. In addition, the city is located in "Tornado Alley" and often experiences violent thunderstorms.

The Thunder didn't make much noise at first. The team lost 29 of its first 32 games in 2008–09. It finished 23–59. It was Westbrook's rookie season, and he showed that he would become a star. Top draft choice shooting guard James Harden joined the team for the 2009–10 season. The Thunder boomed to a 50–32 mark. Durant became the youngest player to win the scoring title. He averaged 30.1 points a game. He was just 21. The Thunder lost to the defending champion Lakers in the first round of the playoffs.

James Harden

Oklahoma City won 55 games the following season. The Thunder easily defeated Denver in the first playoff round. They defeated the Memphis Grizzlies in the next. But they couldn't get past the Dallas Mavericks in the Western Conference finals.

The Thunder had a 47–19 mark in the lockout-shortened 2011–12 season. Only Boston and San Antonio had better records. Oklahoma City swept Dallas in the first round of the playoffs. Then it defeated the Lakers in the second round. The Thunder lost the first two games to the Spurs in the conference finals. They won the next four. "This has kinda been like a Hollywood script for OKC," said Spurs coach Gregg Popovich. "First they played Dallas and then the Lakers and now us. That's 10 of the last 13 championships."

Unfortunately, Miami cooled the storming Thunder in the Finals. Oklahoma City won the first game but lost the next four. LeBron James of the Heat praised the Thunder. "They're going to be a team to be reckoned with for a lot of years … and they're going to use this experience as motivation," he said.

GREAT TALENT, NO TITLE

The Thunder seemed like they were on their way to another meeting with Miami in the 2012–13 season. Their 60–22 record was the best in the Western Conference. But Westbrook suffered a serious knee injury in the first round of the playoffs. Oklahoma City held on to win the series. Without their playmaker and second-leading scorer, they lost to the Memphis Grizzlies in the next round. Oklahoma City was just as good in

Russell Westbrook

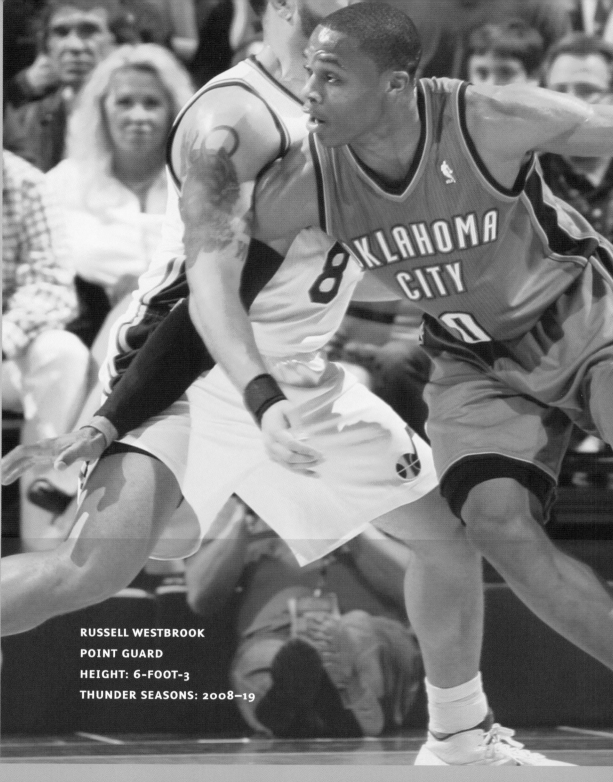

RUSSELL WESTBROOK
POINT GUARD
HEIGHT: 6-FOOT-3
THUNDER SEASONS: 2008–19

HONORING HIS FRIEND'S MEMORY

Growing up in Lawndale, California, best friends Russell Westbrook and Khelcey Barrs III had a dream as they began high school. They wanted to play together in college. There was one problem. The 6-foot-6 Barrs was already drawing attention from college programs. Westbrook was just 5-foot-8. No one was interested in him. Tragically, Barrs died when he was 16 from an undiagnosed heart condition. Westbrook was devastated. He channeled his grief into hard work. "When he passed, it just made me think about life and how every time I step on the floor, I have to give it my all," he said. Their high school coach Chris Young agreed. "Russell is living his dream for his friend. I believe Khelcey's energy is in Russell, pushing him to be the MVP of the NBA." Westbrook wears a bracelet with the inscription KBIII in every game.

OKLAHOMA CITY THUNDER

2013–14. It won 59 games. Durant was named the league's MVP. He averaged 32 points a game. The Thunder advanced to the Western Conference finals. But they lost to the Spurs.

Durant and Westbrook both missed parts of the 2014–15 season with injuries. The Thunder still won 45 games. But the New Orleans Pelicans edged them for the final playoff spot. Oklahoma City surged back in 2015–16. Center Enes Kanter and power forward Serge Ibaka provided scoring and rebounding. The Thunder upset the 67-win Spurs in the conference semifinals. They won three of the first four games in the conference finals against Golden State, which had won an NBA-record 73 games that season. But the Warriors took the next three. Durant left after the season to join Golden State.

The Thunder rode Westbrook's historic triple-double 2016–17 season to a 47–35 mark. Westbrook was named league MVP. They lost in the first round to the Rockets. Oklahoma City added veteran stars Paul George and Carmelo Anthony for the 2017–18 season. The team won 48 games but lost in the first round of the playoffs. The next three seasons were virtually identical—win totals in the mid-to-high 40s, followed by early playoff exits. Aging stars didn't seem to be the answer, as the team couldn't seem to advance to the next level. Anthony lasted just one season, George two.

Westbrook continued to rack up triple-doubles, 25 in 2017–18 and 34 the following season. He also averaged a triple-double per game in both seasons. Yet even he wasn't untouchable. He left in a trade in 2019. In return, the Thunder got Chris Paul. He was traded after the season.

NICK COLLISON
POWER FORWARD/CENTER
HEIGHT: 6-FOOT-10
SONICS/THUNDER SEASONS: 2004–18

"MR. THUNDER"

Nick Collison played his entire 14-year career with the Seattle/Oklahoma City franchise. Teammates and fans called him "Mr. Thunder." He never averaged double digits in points or rebounds in any season. His chief assets were his work ethic and willingness to do whatever it took to win. For example, Collison became one of the league leaders in drawing charging fouls. "I try to have just a little bit quicker anticipation when the drive is coming over," he explained. In 2019, he became the first player with part of his career in Oklahoma City to have his number retired. At the ceremony honoring him, Paul George said, "He was a guy that was always ready, always prepared. Never took a day off."

Shai Gilgeous-Alexander

The Thunder went into full rebuilding mode in the 2020–21 season. They finished 22–50. It was the team's lowest win total since the final year in Seattle. On the other hand, the team was stockpiling draft choices. In addition, veteran shooting/point guard Shai Gilgeous-Alexander averaged more than 20 points game. Small forward Luguentz Dort was called "the highest-effort defensive player in the NBA" while scoring more than 17 points a game.

Oklahoma City continued its emphasis on rebuilding in 2021–22. The team's average age of 22.7 years was younger than some *college* teams. One pitfall came on December 2. The Grizzlies hung a 152–79 beatdown on the Thunder. The 73-point differential is the largest in league history. The team rebounded to win five of its next eight games en route to a final mark of 24–58. The Thunder's top draft choice, 6-foot-8 Josh Giddey, was an instant starter and in February became the youngest player in NBA history with two consecutive triple-doubles. He was just 19 at the time. The Thunder got even younger in 2022-23 with the addition of three lottery picks from the 2022 NBA Draft. With the second overall selection, Oklahoma City selected 7-footer Chet Holmgren out of Gonzaga. He averaged 14 points, 10 rebounds, and nearly 4 blocks a game in his lone collegiate season. Unfortunately, Holmgren injured his foot before the 2022-23 season and was ruled out for the entire season. Oklahoma City acquired the 11th pick Ousmane Dieng from France. With the next selection, they added Jalen Williams from Santa Clara.

The Seattle SuperSonics had a long and proud history before moving to Oklahoma City. The Thunder have lived up to this notable history. Fans hope another championship banner will soon join the one the 1979 Sonics hoisted.

Josh Giddey

INDEX